Prayer Secrets
Keys to a Spirit filled prayer life

by
Dan Vis

All Scripture quotations are from the
King James Version of the Bible
Emphasis supplied unless otherwise indicated.

ISBN: 978-1-958155-02-8

Published by FAST Missions
111 2nd Street
Kathryn, ND 58049

Additional copies of this book are available by
visiting us at WWW.FAST.ST

Dedication

This book is dedicated to a small group of older women, who showed me, at an Oklahoma Campmeeting many years ago, that it truly was possible to pray down an outpouring of the Holy Spirit!

Table of Contents

Prayer Secrets
Preface

I've always been intrigued by the topic of prayer. As a rather analytical, and sometimes philosophical thinker, I've long wrestled with the fact there are impenetrable mysteries connected with prayer that reason alone cannot resolve. Paul was likely thinking of these mysteries when he wrote: "O the depth of the riches both of the wisdom and knowledge of God! How unsearchable are his judgments, and his ways past finding out!" (Romans 11:33).

Of course, that doesn't mean we can't enter into those mysteries practically. In fact, I'm convinced that's the only way we really can learn how to pray—to actually pray. And so, in the pages ahead, I share a step by step plan to help you build an innovative, and even radical sort of prayer journal—not to share all the secrets to prayer, but to show you how you can enter into those secrets yourself, experientially.

If you have tried a prayer journal before with little success, don't let that deter you from pressing ahead. This approach is something unusual. And if you are at all like me, you will quickly discover how prayer impacts back on the one who prays. Or to put it differently, entering the audience chamber of God changes us, far more than it changes Him!

It's my hope, these pages will help you enter into the experience of prayer. And in so doing, learn more how to pray!

Teach us to Pray
Chapter 1

Prayer is one aspect of the Christian life that many find mysterious and strange. We are consistently encouraged to be men and women of prayer, and we may even have a strong desire to grow in our prayer life--but often we don't know how to go about pursuing that. We wish someone would just pull back the curtain, and show us how to pray.

I'm sure the disciples felt that way at times. They saw Jesus rise up early for prayer, spend whole nights in prayer, combine fasting with prayer--and saw the amazing results of answered prayer in His life. No doubt, as they overheard Him pouring out His heart to His Father in heaven, their own hearts were stirred with a desire to enter into that same kind of experience.

How Do You Do It?

The Bible actually recounts one instance where they asked Jesus for a few tips:

Luke 11:1
And it came to pass, that, as he was praying in a
certain place, when he ceased, one of his disciples
said unto him, Lord, teach us to pray, as John
also taught his disciples.

Jesus responded to their request with a model prayer (the Lord's prayer), outlining several priority areas of prayer. Then He shared a parable about the importance of being persistent ("importunity") and a bit of related commentary. I'm sure He taught them other lessons about prayer, at other times as well.

How wonderful it would be to go back in time, to watch Jesus pray, and listen to His teachings on the subject. To ask a few questions and clear up some points. Wouldn't you love to do that?

Problems in Prayer
No doubt those disciples started out just like us, having just as much confusion about how prayer works as we do. Had more of their conversations with Jesus been recorded, we might discover they asked the exact same questions I hear so often today. Perhaps you too have heard these questions, or even asked them yourself:

- How do I know what to pray for? How do I know whether something is God's will or not?
- How do I keep my mind from wandering? Or worse, keep myself from dozing off?
- How do I know God hears me? Why do I feel like I'm talking to a wall?
- How do I avoid forgetting to pray for important things? Especially when people ask me to pray for them?

- How do I persevere in prayer? And how do I know when to stop praying for something?
- How do I claim promises? What does that even mean?
- How do I exercise faith? What is my part in seeing my own prayers answered?

Somehow the twelve found answers to these question, because by Pentecost, they had become powerful in prayer. The Bible reports "these all continued with one accord in prayer and supplication" (Acts 1:14). And the results were impressive: the power of God came crashing in like a "rushing mighty wind" and "they were all filled with the Holy Ghost" (Acts 2:1-4). Clearly, they had learned the secrets to prayer!

Don't you agree we need to re-discover the answers to these questions today?

Prayer in the 21st Century

Like many things in the Christian life, prayer is not something you learn theologically. You need to study it experientially. That is, the best way to grow in prayer--is simply to pray. And as you commune with God, He will answer all these questions personally, in ways that are uniquely meaningful to us individually. Our prayer life will deepen as our relationship with God becomes more intimate.

That doesn't mean, however, a book like this can't help. It can! Because what I'm going to share over the next few days is a simple, practical plan to help get you praying.

In particular I'm going to share a nuts and bolts, step by step strategy for creating your own full-featured prayer journal, and teach you how to use it. Implement these suggestions, and it is sure to strengthen your prayer life. Practice this system over time, and you will find answers to all of those questions above.

And you may just start seeing more answers to your prayers. And maybe even a bit more of the Holy Spirit's presence in your life!

But it will only work if you act on these suggestions. And that's because the only way to really grow in prayer, is to pray.

So get ready. In our next section, I'll show you exactly how to get started.

Study Questions
Chapter 1

List the seven most common questions people ask about prayer at the beginning of this chapter?

■

■

■

■

■

■

■

Which of these questions do you struggle with most?

What is the best way to learn the secrets to prayer?

What is the only way a training resource like this can help?

Additional Notes:

Ask of Me
Chapter 2

Prayer is a curious topic. It's so simple, the smallest child can do it. Yet there are questions so profound, they perplex the most learned theologians. But the essential questions can all be answered, if you will do one thing: pray. Actually, there's no other way to really learn it. You come to understand prayer by praying.

Over the next few days, I want to share a simple way to pray using a specific kind of prayer journal I was taught to use many years ago. If you follow the suggestions I'm going to introduce, it will help you discover experientially, answers to all the most important questions about prayer that people ask.

Why a Prayer Journal?

Just like it helps to follow some plan when doing Bible study, and to have a good system when memorizing Scripture, a little structure can strengthen your prayer life too. This is especially true when first starting out. And just as with Bible study and Scripture memory, the benefits of a little structure will actually compound with time! If you stick with it.

A prayer journal provides that structure.

There are other benefits as well, that will become more clear as we implement the suggestions I give. You will discover it helps you remember to pray for important requests, and prioritize them properly. It will help you connect requests to specific promises. It can help ensure the subjects you pray about remain balanced. It will show you how to persevere in prayer, cooperate with God in working to see your requests answered, and help you to track answered prayers.

Believe it or not, a simple prayer journal system can do all this and more!

The Essentials

The first step in organizing your prayer journal is to get a small loose leaf notebook. If you already have a notebook that you use for Bible study notes and applications, you can use the same notebook. But it absolutely needs to be loose leaf, so you can add and remove pages, or move them around.

You'll also need some paper. You'll use these to begin inserting requests into your prayer journal--one request to a page. We'll talk more about how to organize these sheets later in this book, but you have to have a few requests in your prayer journal before you can start organizing them, so let's start here.

A loose leaf binder and some pages. Plus a pen or pencil. And a Bible. These are the essentials...

The First Request

Each day through this course, I'm going to give you some action assignments. Remember, the goal is not to teach you theory, but to help you learn through doing. Your assignment for today, after grabbing your notebook, paper, and other supplies, is to write out your first prayer request.

Here are the basic steps:

Take a few moments to identify a pressing prayer concern. It can be anything. Tomorrow, I'll talk more about how to know what to pray for, but anything that is a burden on your heart is fair game. Whisper a quick prayer for the Holy Spirit to bring something important to mind.

Once you have it, take out a sheet of paper. Write today's date at the top of the page. Then below that, write the word "Request", and then the actual request in your own words. Keep it simple and concise.

Skip a line, then write the word "Scriptures". If you can think of a relevant verse or promise that makes it clear this request is in harmony with God's Word, write it down. If not leave it blank. You can always add verses later, at any time.

Skip another few lines (to leave room for any relevant verses you find later) and write the word "Notes". You'll use this section to record the dates you pray for this request, as well as notes about how you observe God working in answer to this request. I'll explain more how to use this section later. For now, simply commit this request to God in prayer, and then write down today's date at the top of this final section of the page.

Congratulations! You've just written your first prayer request, and begun using your prayer journal. Great job! If you have time, feel free to add a few more requests. But don't add too many just yet, however. I will talk more about how to know what requests to add in the next chapter.

You are welcome to print our our free prayer request sheets and use them if you like. They are completely free to members of our community (*http://fast.st/pjform*). We've also got a digital prayer journal you can use that works as described in this class. If you are a gadget kind of person, be sure to check that out as well! (*http://fast.st/prayer*).

The Power of a Prayer

Since we're just getting started, let me tell you a story about the power of a simple prayer request sheet.

I wasn't a Christian when I first went to college, and my freshman year was a bit wild. But I had a few friends in my dorm who were committed Christians, and I was attracted to their lives. One in particular, was another freshman named Rod. He lived right across the hall from me, and he was a wonderful witness that entire year.

Unfortunately, I wasn't ready to make a commitment myself, and ended up dropping out of college for a year to "find myself". After a few twists and turns, I ended up finding Christ instead, and went back to that same college the next year as a freshly baptized believer. One of the first things I did was look up my old friend Rod to tell him the news.

When I dropped by his apartment and told him I was a Christian, a surprised look came over his face, and then a giant smile. He invited me in and asked me to wait a moment while he went to get something. He came back with a small loose leaf binder, from which he took out a single sheet of paper.

At the top was a date, and then a request for my conversion. That was followed by a number of Bible promises, and then line after line of dates representing all the times he had prayed for me. In fact the dates filled the whole front page, and much of the back.

I'm not sure who was more shocked: me seeing all those prayers on my behalf, or him seeing all those prayers answered! But we both rejoiced in a God who answers prayer, together!

Soon your prayer journal is going to have requests just like that. And you are going to see results just as miraculous. But it all starts with your first request. What will it be?

Next, we'll look at how to know what to pray for...

Study Questions
Chapter 2

In addition to providing structure, what other benefits does a prayer journal provide:

Why is it essential to use a loose leaf notebook for your prayer journal?

What are the four sections you should include on each prayer request sheet?

■

■

■

■

What will the first (or next) prayer request be that you add to your prayer journal?

Additional Notes:

Hid in a Field
Chapter 3

We're just getting started in this class, but we've made some good progress already. If you have been keeping up with our action steps, you have obtained a loose leaf binder for your new prayer journal. And, you've written out your first prayer request. Perhaps a few. And you've even recorded the date you first prayed over those requests.

Today we're going to take the next step, and talk about how to know what requests to put in your prayer journal. Or to put it differently, how do we know what God wants us to ask?

The Usual Methods

There are at least two common approaches people use when picking requests to put in their prayer journal.

First, people gravitate toward the pressures in their life. If they face some problem, have some need, struggle with some difficulty--these come to mind quickly. It's normal to go to God for relief from the challenges in our life.

And it's biblical. The Bible clearly tells us to "be careful for nothing" and instead present those needs to God "by prayer and supplication" (Philippians 4:6). God longs for us to bring these needs to him, and put our trust in Him. Or as Peter describes it, we are to cast "all your care upon him; for he careth for you" (I Peter 5:7).

The second approach is to fill their prayer journal with requests for prayer from friends and family. Just as we want to bring our needs to God, loved ones will sometimes ask for prayer, and will feel comfort knowing you are interceding with God on their behalf.

And this is biblical as well. Paul urges us to "bear ye one another's burdens" (Galatians 6:2). James urges us to "pray one for another" (James 5:16). Samuel, in fact, saw this as a moral duty: "Moreover as for me, God forbid that I should sin against the LORD in ceasing to pray for you" (I Samuel 12:23).

Clearly, both of these approaches have their place, and you will likely want to include both kinds of requests in your prayer journal. However, there's a limitation to this approach.

The fact is, we don't always know how God plans to use the troubles in our life. And neither do those friends asking for our prayer. Paul put it this way: "we know not what we should pray for as we ought" (Romans 8:26). And that's a problem if we are serious about wanting to pray according to God's will.

Finding Treasure

I believe the best requests to add to your prayer journal, are the ones God impresses you to add. And if we start seeking this kind of guidance in the Word, He will do just that.

It reminds me of a parable Jesus once told in the book of Matthew. I don't think He was talking about prayer specifically, but it illustrates the process well:

Matthew 13:44
Again, the kingdom of heaven is like unto treasure hid in a field; the which when a man hath found, he hideth, and for joy thereof goeth and selleth all that he hath, and buyeth that field.

The Bible is like a field, filled with hidden treasure just under the surface. These treasures include amazing principles, commands, and promises. And we stumble on to them as we walk through the field in our daily study. Whenever we find something important--we should determine to gain possession of it. That happens through prayer.

So imagine one day you are studying through the Word of God and you come across some promise. The Holy Spirit calls your attention to it, and speaks to you about some area of need in your life. And you discern what God wants to do for you. Whenever this happens, write out a prayer request asking God to fulfil that very promise, being sure to note the reference in the "Scriptures" section of the prayer request sheet. You just found treasure!

Or maybe you stumble on to some command. The Holy Spirit convicts you, that you could do better implementing those instructions in your life. So you write out a prayer request asking God to strengthen that area of your life--noting any specific changes you feel impressed to make. And of course, you jot down the reference on the prayer request sheet, once again. More treasure.

Another day you find some small bit of wisdom, and the Holy Spirit connects it to some tough decision you are facing. It gives you discernment about the correct course of action. So you fill out another prayer request asking God to bless that decision, to guide you in its implementation, to honor your efforts. Once more, you note the reference. God has given you treasure still again.

Cart Before the Horse

There's nothing wrong with bringing our burdens to the Lord, or praying for loved ones in difficult situations. We should do both, and you are encouraged to include those kinds of requests in your prayer journal as the Lord leads.

But often it's like putting the cart before the horse. We write out our request, hoping it's God will. And then rifle through our memory banks to see if we can't find some relevant Bible promise to slap on it. If we have a promise book, we pull it off the shelf, and look up healing or loneliness or guidance, turn to the appropriate page, and grab some promise from there. That has always seemed a rather backward approach to me.

Why not study the Bible first. Let the Holy Spirit impress you with the things you should pray about. Let your requests flow from the Scriptures themselves, rather than the other way around. Put the horse before the cart!

Actually, you don't have to worry about your personal struggles. If you ask God to speak about them in your devotions, He will. And through that process, God will tell you exactly how He wants you to pray about each need.

And the same thing will happen with your friends. As you study, God will bring certain people to mind through the verses you read. He will give you insights into what He is doing in their life, and show you how best to pray for them.

By putting Scripture first, both your personal prayer needs and the prayer needs of your friends will be met. Trust Him to show you exactly how to pray!

For your action item today, I simply want to encourage you to spend a little time studying the Bible. Ask God to give you one clear prayer request. Then write out a prayer request sheet, jot down the verse, and commit it to God with a prayer. If you have time, pray over any other prayer requests previously entered in your journal as well. Be sure to jot down today's date in the "Notes" section of any sheets you pray over.

We'll talk more about the "Notes" part of our prayer journal system in our next section!

Study Questions
Chapter 3

What is the typical order most people use when it comes to choosing requests to pray for, and finding promises to go with them?

Why is it better to reverse that order?

Give examples from the reading of types of verses you can transform into prayer requests:

Why do we not have to worry about neglecting requests for our own needs, and the needs of friends when choosing to seek requests in Scripture first?

Spend some time in the Bible today, looking for prayer requests sparked by the passage you read.

What passage did you read:

What request did it spark:

Additional Notes:

Walking with God
Chapter 4

Ready to dig deeper in our study of Prayer Secrets? So far we've talked about how to get started with a prayer journal, how to write out individual prayer requests, and how to know what things to pray for. And hopefully you've begun using your prayer journal as well.

Today we're going to look at one of the most important keys to an effective prayer journal. I call it "Walking with God".

Good Old Enoch

One of the best verses in the Bible to illustrate the concept I want to talk about is this curious verse from the book of Genesis:

Genesis 5:24
And Enoch walked with God: and he was not; for
God took him.

If there was ever a man to understand prayer, it must have been Enoch. He grew so close to God, he ended up being translated to heaven without seeing death. Hebrews puts it this way:

Hebrews 11:5
By faith Enoch was translated that he should not
see death; and was not found, because God had
translated him: for before his translation he had
this testimony, that he pleased God.

Putting a few things together, it seems clear faith pleases God. In fact, "without faith it is impossible to please him" (Hebrews 11:6). In the life of Enoch, that faith is represented by him walking with God. Intimately.

Somehow, we too need to learn to do this, practically. Today we'll be looking at the subject of faith, and how to incorporate it into your prayer journal.

Faith and Works

There has been an ongoing debate for centuries about the proper relationship between faith and works. And we're certainly not going to settle that issue here. But I do want to spend a few moments talking about works in relation to prayer.

Faith, of course, is indispensable to prayer. Jesus clearly taught this when He said: "all things are possible to him that believeth" (Mark 9:23). And then again more explicitly: "What things soever ye desire, when ye pray, believe that ye receive them, and ye shall have them" (Mark 11:24).

The book of James, in contrast, talks about prayers which lack faith: "But let him ask in faith, nothing wavering. For he that wavereth is like a wave of the sea driven with the wind and tossed. For let not that man think that he shall receive any thing of the Lord." (James 1:6-7).

In other words, the requests in your prayer journal, even if rooted in Scripture, must be "mixed with faith" if you want to see them answered (Hebrews 4:2).

Now faith is simply believing God will do what He says. But the evidence of faith is a willingness to act in harmony with that belief. Quoting James once again:

James 2:17
Even so faith, if it hath not works, is dead, being alone.

To put it differently, action reveals a living faith. Inaction suggests a faith that is weak, or worse. If we want to see the requests in our prayer journal answered, we need to do more than just trust God will do it. We need to add a bit of action.

This process of learning to cooperate with God in working to answer our own requests, turns each prayer request into a bit of an adventure. Each becomes a personal journey with God. Or as I like to think of it--it's walking with God.

Taking Notes
The key to doing this, involves learning to use the "Notes" section of your prayer request sheet effectively.

The beginning step is simply remembering to record the date each time you pray. This gives you a log of the various times you discuss each request with God. Some of your requests may one day have dozens or even hundreds of dates. Like the friend begging bread (Luke 11:5-8) or the widow who kept visiting the unjust judge (Luke 18:1-6), having a prayer journal can help you persevere in presenting your requests to God.

But there is much more to this than just recording dates.
As you pray over each request, take time to listen as well. Ask God if there is anything He would have you do that day to cooperate with Him in answering the request. I personally believe prayer is more about listening than speaking. And in my experience, God often brings specific tasks to mind instantly, if

I will but ask Him. When God speaks to you like this, use the notes section to jot those instructions down.

If you have a time management system, you should record the task there as well, to help ensure it gets carried out.

There are other things God may show you about your requests if you ask Him. He may bring to mind small things that have happened which indicate He is working to answer the request. Jot those observations down. He may give you a deeper understanding of His will regarding that request. Jot those insights down as well. He may even highlight some verse connected to the request. Jot it down here, as well, or add it to the "Scriptures" section. And if God fully answers the request, or it becomes clear His answer is no, jot that down as well. I'll talk more about answered prayers another day.

In other words, the notes section should not just be a log of dates. You want it to be a log of the whole journey. All the interactions between you and God as you pray over that request. It's a record of your walk with God.

Want to see a sample of what a filled in sheet looks like? Check out this sample prayer request sheet for a better idea how it all works. (*http://fast.st/pjsample*).

Try It Out

Learn to use the "Notes" section of your Prayer Journal, and it can transform your prayer life. It's a powerful way to mix a bit of faith into your requests, by adding some action. Perhaps more important, it changes prayer from one way to two way communication. Why not give it a try?

In fact, that's your action step for today. Add another request or two, as God puts them on your heart. Especially, look for requests triggered during your personal devotions. And pray over these requests, as well as any others already in your journal.

But rather than just recording the date, listen a bit. And see if God doesn't speak to you about one or more of your requests, give you some insight, show you what He's doing, assign you some task. Don't pause too long on any one request, or expect Him to talk to you about every request, every day. Just pause a moment, and invite the Spirit to speak--then date your request and move on to the next one. And of course, if He does impress something on your heart, jot that down as well. In other words, practice documenting where your time with God takes you each day.

Next, we'll look at how to stay balanced in prayer...

Study Questions
Chapter 4

How did Enoch demonstrate faith?

What are four things we should understand about the relationship between faith and works:

- Faith is _____ to prayer.

- Faith is believing God will _____.

- _____ reveals a living faith.

- Faith involves learning to _____ with God.

Explain how to use the "Notes" section to turn each request into a personal journey with God:

What kinds of things do you anticipate would happen if we spent more time listening for God to speak and prayer, and we acted on what God said?

Additional Notes:

Staying Balanced
Chapter 5

So far, we've been introducing the various building blocks of our prayer journal system. And hopefully you've begun to get an idea how it works. We still have a few important details to cover related to how you organize your prayer journal, and we'll do that tomorrow. But today I want to spend a bit of time talking about the importance of balance in prayer.

The information we cover today will help to ensure you have a good healthy mix of requests in your prayer journal.

Strange Patterns

I've noticed a few strange patterns over the years, about the kinds of things people pray for. Maybe you've noticed some of these yourself.

If you are in a typical prayer service, where prayer requests are solicited publically, you will probably notice 75% or more of the prayer requests are for friends struggling with some health challenge. It's almost as if that's our number one concern as Christians. While the Bible does encourage prayer for the sick, it's certainly not the overarching theme of the Bible. And eliminating sickness is not the primary mission of the church.

Once a person gets to their private prayer closet, the requests seem to change. More often than not, they deal with financial pressures. Praying for a new job, a raise, the ability to pay some bill, or make some desired purchase. Again, there's nothing wrong with presenting these kinds of needs to God in prayer, but prayer is much more than simply accessing an endless ATM in the sky.

I've known some people who spend the majority of their prayer time in deep introspection, overwhelmed by their sin, earnest in confession, deep in remorse and repentance. Others seem to go to the opposite extreme. Their prayers are jam-packed with nothing but praise, thanksgiving, and celebration.

Seems like everyone is trying to ride a unicycle. Where's the balance in all that?

The Lord's Prayer

When Jesus was asked by His disciples to give them some tips on prayer (Luke 11:1), He responded by giving them two tips. First, He taught them a model prayer (Luke 11:2-4), often referred to today as the Lord's Prayer. Second, he taught them the importance of perseverance and determination (Luke 11:5-8). Or to use the Bible's word: importunity.

A prayer journal can definitely help with the stick-to-it part of praying over your requests. But today I want to talk about how a prayer journal can help you also achieve greater balance.

You see, I think we've missed the point Jesus was trying to make in giving us the Lord's Prayer. Matthew's version, which is the more familiar one, is immediately preceded by this warning:

Matthew 6:7
But when ye pray, use not vain repetitions, as the
heathen do: for they think that they shall be heard
for their much speaking.

Thousands have skipped right over these words. They memorize those next few verses, and then recite them at every opportunity. But it seems quite likely, that Jesus had something very different in mind. I believe He was simply suggesting a balance in the things we pray for.

Suggested Topics
Actually, the Bible is filled with sample prayers, as well as explicit instructions to pray for specific things. Studying through the Bible will give you no end of subjects to pray over. But considering Jesus began His instructions about prayer with this model prayer, it seems appropriate we at least make sure we hit all the main topics here, when launching our prayer journal. Here's the Lord's Prayer:

Matthew 6:9-12
9 After this manner therefore pray ye: Our Father
which art in heaven, Hallowed be thy name. 10
Thy kingdom come, Thy will be done in earth, as
it is in heaven. 11 Give us this day our daily
bread. 12 And forgive us our debts, as we forgive
our debtors.

I see at least a half dozen topics. You might break things down differently, but the list below is just a suggestion to help you get started:

Worship: Hallowed be thy name

Be sure to include one or more requests dedicated to praising God for His various attributes. And perhaps another request dedicated to giving thanks. You can make the initial request a bit general, then use the notes section to jot down different attributes to praise Him for each day, or different things you're thankful for. It's easy to skip worship and jump right into our needs. Having a few "worship" type requests can help prevent that.

Guidance: Thy will be done

Your prayer journal should also include requests for guidance. I like to formulate these requests as a specific question about which of two or more options is best. And then in the notes section I jot down verses and other insights that suggest one answer or the other. Eventually, I gain clarity as to God's will and peace I have discerned it correctly. At that point I can then move on to formulating a plan of action and shift my prayers toward seeking His strength and blessing.

Provision: Give us ... our daily bread

We should present our needs to God in prayer. But don't limit this to financial needs. Present important physical, social, relational, and spiritual needs to God as well. And the word "us" suggests we should lift up the needs of others as well. God longs to provide for His children, but I believe we miss out on many of those blessings because we do not ask for that provision.

Forgiveness: Forgive us our debts

It's probably a good idea to add a request or two that reminds you to review your recent actions, and see if there has been some area of failure or disobedience. If something comes to mind, ask forgiveness. Confession cleanses the soul from guilt. If you sense resentment toward some person, add a request for God to change your heart. Praying blessings for our enemies, as Jesus instructed, is a powerful way to wash away bitter feelings.

Victory: Lead us not into temptation

Just before his arrest in the Garden of Gethsemane, Jesus explained the power of prayer to strengthen us when facing temptation. And we still need that power today, don't we? I recommend identifying two or three specific areas of your life that you struggle with, and write up a specific prayer request for each. Use the "Notes" section to record insights to overcoming. Keep praying until you understand what you need to obtain full victory! Then choose another area to work on.

Protection: Deliver us from evil

We live in a dangerous world, and I suspect angels protect us from harm more often than we know. But having a few requests for protection included in your prayer journal is a good idea. In particular, if you have worries about something in your immediate future, commit it to God in prayer. Maybe a trip. A health concern. Prayer for a son or daughter. Through prayer you can fortify every facet of your life.

Submission: For thine is the kingdom

Ultimately, our prayers should focus in on the advance of God's kingdom. To encourage this, add requests for specific people you would like to see come to Christ. New Christians (by name) who may be struggling spiritually. Workers in your church, ministries (like FAST), and missionaries serving in various countries. Perhaps most important of all, add a request for God to strengthen your own personal commitment to the Great Commission.

Off the Unicycle

Take a few moments to assess the kinds of requests in your prayer journal, and see if you notice a pattern. Compare it with the types of things Jesus encouraged us to pray about in His model prayer. Are there areas that are missing? Areas where your requests seem overly concentrated? If so, it's time to make an adjustment.

For your action item today, my recommendation is to write out at least one request for each of the categories above not currently represented in your prayer journal.

You may also wish to think about the order you arrange these requests. You don't have to follow the steps in this prayer exactly, but you may find it helpful to group similar requests, and start being a bit more structured in how you order them. This is one advantage of a loose leaf notebook. You can reorder requests at any time.

Note also that these are not the only categories, by any means. There are, in fact, many other things we are explicitly told to pray about in the Bible. But since Jesus started here, it seems as good a place as any to start pursuing balance. You can add as many more requests as you like on any topics you wish, in the months and years to come. Just assess those requests every once in a while, to make sure your list is somewhat, well, balanced. :)

In our next section, we'll talk about the surprising problem people experience once they first begin getting serious about a prayer journal.

Study Questions
Chapter 5

When Jesus was asked by His disciples to give them some tips on prayer, He gave them two tips. What were they?

■

■

What seven topics are suggested in the Lord's Prayer as key to a balanced prayer life?

■

■

■

■

■

■

■

Evaluate your prayer life. What areas seem weak? What areas seem strong?

What can you do to experience more balance?

Additional Notes:

Tough Decisions
Chapter 6

If you have been following along with our instructions so far, you should have a pretty good idea how our prayer journal system works. And maybe you've even begun to appreciate some of the benefits.

- Connecting requests to promises
- Staying focused longer
- Adding action to your faith
- Having more balance in prayer
- Growing in perseverance
- Remembering friends' requests

Perhaps you can think of more. Certainly you've solved one of the most common difficulties: running out of things to say. Once you have a fair number of requests, praying over them individually and listening for God to speak back can easily fill any time slots you have available for prayer. But it also introduces another issue. How do I find time to pray for everything?

Organizing Requests

It is not a trivial problem. If you are committing the trials of your life to prayer, faithfully praying for friends that ask it, and finding new requests in your devotional study on a regular basis--it's only a matter of time before your prayer journal will start filling up. And even more so if you are intentional about having requests in every key category!

I found a simple solution that worked for me.

Add some tabs to your prayer journal, and begin organizing your requests. There's more than one way to do this, but the approach I liked best was to have one tab for priority requests and another for regular requests. With that, you just divide your requests into the two categories, and insert them behind the appropriate tabs. You will also probably want to have a tab for answered prayers, and perhaps one for closed requests.

When you pray, try to work through the priority requests first. I recommend keeping the number of requests here to a minimum--no more than 10 or 20. Try to pray through these requests every day. After all, these are your highest priority!

Then, with any remaining time, pray through a portion of your regular requests. Put a bookmark where you finish, and pick up where you leave off the next time you pray. When you get to the end, start over again at the beginning.

If God impresses you to pray about a specific request one day, feel free to do so. Even if it means doing things out of order. Your journal is meant to help you, not restrict you. Just be sure to jot down the date and make a note. Something important may be about to happen!

Of course, if you work through these regular requests in order, you will pray over every request consistently, even if it takes a week or two to get through them all. And all the while, you will be giving your priority requests a strong daily focus.

Our online prayer journal tool allows you to organize your requests into daily, weekly, monthly, and even quarterly requests. This gives you the added advantage of being able to further define how you prioritize each request. And there's no reason you can't do this in a paper prayer journal as well. It does require you to spend time in multiple categories and adds the pressure of trying to pray through each section to the end within the specified time periods. But it's an option to consider. Our online prayer journal manages all of this automatically.

Making Choices

Either way, however, there's a surprise benefit to the prioritization process. It forces you to try and tune in to the will of God. The requests that are most important to God, should be most important to you--and prayed over more frequently. Those that are not so important, can be prayed over less often.

Which suggests that another important aspect of your prayer time is asking God whether a request needs to be moved up or down. While it may feel awkward to have to make these kinds of decisions at first, I've found it actually quite valuable. It forces me to ask God difficult questions, and make tough choices. Over time, the things most important to God rise to the top, and my priorities shift into closer alignment with God's. Your prayer journal becomes a living, growing, reflection of your deepening understanding of God's will.

Which is another important insight to prayer. While many view prayer as a way to change God and get Him to do the things we want, the opposite is actually true. Prayer is designed to change us, so we can more fully pursue the things that God wants. Making tough decisions about which requests deserve our best attention is one way that happens.

Nuts and Bolts

So how does all this work? It's pretty simple actually. As you pray through your prayer journal each day, keep one spiritual ear open to God's voice, and the possibility He might want you to change the frequency of a prayer request. If He does, just move it.

If a request has been answered, either yes or no, move it to the answered prayer tab for future reference. Looking back over your answered prayers can be a great source of encouragement to you.

If you no longer feel a burden to pray over a request you can move it to the tab for closed requests. In general, it is a good idea to pray for a request as long as you believe it to be God's will, until that prayer is answered. But there may be situations, when you feel impressed to pray for a certain topic for a certain period of time--as an application from your Bible study, for example. So if you decide to pray for patience for exactly one week, you can remove it at the end of seven days. Or if you want to commit one month to praying for a plan to eliminate debt, or to become a better witness, give your request those thirty days, then close it. You can note any expiration date God impresses upon you right below the start date at the top of the request sheet.

It may also happen God simply releases you from some of your requests. Using our system, you will be constantly adding new requests. There's nothing wrong with removing old requests anytime you wish.

That's part of the transformation process too, isn't it? Filtering out older requests and replacing them with new ones, as your circumstances change, and your understanding of God's will for your life deepens. Let your prayer journal grow with you.

Ok, so much for organizing your prayer journal. Your action step today is simply to get some tabs and organize your requests as described above. From here on out it's up to you to choose your topics, write out prayer request sheets, organize them how you wish, and pray over them.

One more reading still to go. In it we'll talk about going beyond your prayer journal, and entering into deeper, and even more intimate prayer experiences.

Study Questions
Chapter 6

What is the only way to find time to pray for everything we want to pray for?

Today's study recommends creating what four tabs in your prayer journal:

■

■

■

■

Explain how to use priority and regular sections of your prayer journal:

What is one surprise benefit of prioritizing requests?

Additional Notes:

Pressing Closer
Chapter 7

Wow, hard to believe we've come to the end of our Prayer Secrets book. You now have all the basic information you need to create and use our prayer journal system effectively. And if you've been keeping up with all our action items, your prayer journal is already taking shape and getting some use. Kudos!

Today is our last day, and I've got just a few closing tips. Then we're done!

Quick Review

You may remember I talked about some of the common problems people face when first learning to pray. Here were some of the ones I listed:

- How do I know what to pray for? How do I know whether something is God's will or not?
- How do I keep my mind from wandering? Or worse, keep myself from dozing off?
- How do I know God hears me? Why do I feel like I'm talking to a wall?

- How do I avoid forgetting to pray for important things? Especially when people ask me to pray for them?
- How do I persevere in prayer? And how do I know when to stop praying for something?
- How do I claim promises? What does that even mean?
- How do I exercise faith? What is my part in seeing my own prayers answered?

Now that we are at the end of the course, I want you to look back over the list again. If you have been practicing the tips I've shared each day, you are probably already getting insights into the answers for all these questions.

A prayer journal is a powerful tool because it helps you learn the secrets to prayer, experientially. And prayer, as I've said before, is more easily learned by actually praying, than by any other means.

Moving Beyond

But with what we've covered so far, we've barely scratched the surface. Prayer goes far beyond just having a good prayer journal.

Much like a good review system is indispensable to effective memorization, regular use of a prayer journal is foundational to effective prayer. But real memorization doesn't stop with 20 minutes of review each day. There's fresh memorization and meditation all through the day. Exciting discoveries, adventures in application, opportunities to share. Your daily review just helps make the life of memorization possible.

In the same way, a prayer journal is a tool to strengthen your prayer muscles. Praying faithfully over requests each morning will lead to deeper insights to prayer, and lots of answered requests. But real prayer takes place all through the day, in all kinds of situations and circumstances. Just as daily review leads to meditation "day and night", a prayer journal contributes to prayer "without ceasing". It helps make a life of continual intercession possible.

In other words, a prayer journal is a foundational step in the pursuit of even deeper communion with God.

Personal Communion

There are lots of ways to go further. Here are a few suggestions.

First and foremost, don't let your prayer journal hinder personal conversations with God. If you sense Him tugging on your heart to talk to Him directly about some subject, don't hesitate. Your goal is not to make it through every request, but to cultivate the discipline of prayer. Your prayer journal will still be there after you spend that time with God.

Another idea is to explore ways to use more Scripture in prayer. I personally like to conclude my daily Bible study each morning with a season of prayer, discussing whatever principles and applications I have found that morning. It's a great way to review what God has showed me, and commit myself to carrying out His instructions

Another approaches is to take some specific passage relevant to your needs, and work through it verse by verse, using each verse as a framework for your conversation with God. Passages like the Lord's prayer, the 10 commandments, the love chapter, the spiritual armor, and many others are well suited to this kind of prayer. Try experimenting with this, and start a list of favorite passages somewhere in your prayer journal.

Many people enjoy prayer walking. There are different ways to do this. Some entail walking through a neighborhood and praying for every house they pass by. But it's just as valuable to take a walk in the park and focus that time on talking with God. There is something about all the sunshine, fresh air, and increased circulation, that makes this kind of prayer special. Plus, it makes me think of Enoch!

I have a section in my prayer journal for periodic strategy sessions with God. I'll simply set aside some time and write out a prayer to God, in a form similar to a letter, about whatever the most important issues are in my life at that time. I don't follow any format other than to throw in a date, and I keep my notes for later review--but these sessions have been instrumental in helping me discern God's direction at multiple critical junctures in my life. I probably have hundreds of these pages going back three decades, and it is fascinating to track how the Lord has led me through all those years.

Group prayer can also be powerful. Find a few friends with a burden for prayer and learn how to engage in conversational prayer. It's an approach that makes it easy for a group to pray together. Each person says just a sentence or two, and the "conversation" goes from person to person, in any order as the Holy Spirit leads. Another option is to pray with people by phone. There are probably prayer lines available in your area if you ask around, and these can be very rewarding as well.

One last suggestion is to schedule periodic retreats for extended prayer. They can be as short as an afternoon or run several days. Having long periods to focus on study, memorization, and prayer at important transitional points in your life can be transformative. Sometimes these are combined with fasting, and may focus on a special issue--but they can also be times to just enjoy some extra communion with God. I especially like using these to do long range planning for my life.

No doubt you can think of other ways to pray that have been a blessing to you...

Wrapping Things Up

In conclusion, while there are lots of ways to expand and develop your prayer life, it all starts with an effective prayer journal. Think of that daily time in your prayer journal as foundational to growing in prayer. Just know it doesn't stop there!

Begin with a loose leaf notebook. Put the date, your request, relevant Scriptures on each page, and leave room for notes. Include requests for your personal needs, and the needs of friends and family--but focus on requests triggered by Bible study. Keep your requests balanced, with at least a few in each key area the Bible encourages. And organize them into priority and regular requests, or some similar system, that helps keep your list manageable. Spend at least a few minutes each day praying, asking God for actions to help answer each prayer, and record any insights God gives you. Continue adjusting, tweaking, and fine-tuning your prayer journal until you have it just how you want. And celebrate every answered prayer!

It's a simple process, but it works. Stick with it over time, and all those questions that make prayer so mysterious and strange will begin to get answered. Enjoy...

Study Questions
Chapter 7

Using what you learned these last few days, how would you answer each of these questions which were raised at the beginning of this class:

- How do I know what to pray for?

- How do I keep my mind from wandering?

- How do I know God hears me?

- How do I avoid forgetting to pray for important things?

- How do I persevere in prayer?

- How do I claim promises?

- How do I exercise faith?

What are some of the advanced prayer techniques suggested in this reading to deepen your prayer life further?

Why is it recommended that you keep regular time in a prayer journal as foundational to your prayer life?

Additional Notes:

FAST Missions
Cutting-Edge Tools and Training

Ready to become a Revival Agent? FAST Missions can help! Our comprehensive training curriculum will give you the skills you need to take in God's Word effectively, live it out practically, and pass it on to others consistently.

Eager to start memorizing God's Word? Our powerful keys will transform your ability to hide Scripture in your heart.

Want to explore the secrets of "real life" discipleship? Our next level training zooms in on critical keys to growth, like Bible study, prayer, time management, and more.

Want to become a worker in the cause of Christ? Our most advanced training is designed to give you the exact ministry skills you need to see revival spread.

For more information, please visit us at:
WWW.FASTMISSIONS.COM

Study Guides

Looking for life-changing study guides to use in your small group or Bible study class? These resources have been used by thousands around the world. You could be next!

Survival Kit

Want to learn how to memorize Scripture effectively? These study guides will teach you 10 keys to memorization, all drawn straight from the Bible. Our most popular course ever!

Basic Training

Discover nuts and bolts keys to the core skills of discipleship: prayer, Bible study, time management, and more. Then learn how to share these skills with others. It is the course that launched our ministry!

Revival Keys

Now as never before, God's people need revival. And these guides can show you how to spark revival in your family, church, and community. A great revival is coming. Are you ready?

Online Classes

Want to try out some of the resources available at FAST? Here is just a small sampling of courses from among dozens of personal and small group study resources:

Crash Course
Discover Bible-based keys to effective memorization.
http://fast.st/cc

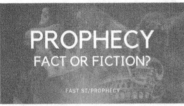

Fact or Fiction
Does the Bible really predict future events? You be the judge.
http://fast.st/prophecy

Monkey Business
Find out how evolution flunks the science test.
http://fast.st/monkey

Dry Bones
Want more of God's Spirit? Learn how to pursue revival.
http://fast.st/bones

The Lost Art
Rediscover New Testament keys to making disciples.
http://fast.st/lostart

Digital Tools

FAST offers a number of powerful "apps for the soul" you can use to grow in your walk with God. And many of these are completely free to anyone with an account. Some of these include:

Memory Engine
Our powerful review engine is designed to help ensure effective longterm Bible memorization. Give it a try, it works!

Bible Reading
An innovative Bible reading tool to help you read through the entire Bible, at your own pace, and in any order you want.

Prayer Journal
Use this tool to organize important requests, and we'll remind you to pray for them on the schedule you want.

Time Management
Learn how to be more productive, by keeping track of what you need to do and when. Just log in daily and get stuff done.

For more information about more than twenty tools like these, please visit us at *http://fast.st/tools*.

Books

If the content of this little book stirred your heart, look for these titles by the same author.

For Such A Time...
A challenging look at the importance of memorization for the last days, including topics such as the Three Angel's messages and the Latter Rain.

Moral Machinery
Discover how our spiritual, mental, and physical faculties work together using the sanctuary as a blueprint. Astonishing insights that could revolutionize your life!

The Movement
Discover God's plan to finish the work through a powerful endtime movement. Gain critical insights into what lies just ahead for the remnant!

Made in the USA
Middletown, DE
03 May 2022

65082043R00036